To Debbie my friend
"The Joy Is Real
Love
Kay Lazenby

UNEVEN EDGES

Kathryn Woodard Lazenby

EVEREADY PRESS
1817 Broadway . Nashville, Tennessee 37203
615-327-9106

Book design by Eveready Press

All paintings are by Kathryn Lazenby

Printed in the USA

ISBN: 978-0-9814694-9-2

Dedication

I dedicate these thoughts
to
Kathryn and Ben Woodard
and
Annie Campbell.
They blessed my life with
Joyful Laughter
and
Humble Wisdom
and
Complete Love

*Annie Campbell
with Harriet Zachry*

Preface

We each walk the Bridge of Our Becoming and dance to the music of our soul. Some days are filled with painful Uneven Edges – We tremble under the edges of loss, of loneliness, of pain, of fear, of random cruel words, unsteady strength, and ever ebbing hope –

In these times of darkness, God's shining grace has given me light for my thoughts, words to express what is in my heart, and a voice to describe what I see in His world – God blessed my journey with loving parents, a wise aunt, beautiful children, treasured friends, and exciting encounters with others on this life journey –

Each day opens as a fragrant bud and each petal unfolds as the hours go by. At the end of the day there is a full blown rose to put upon my pillow and a sweet aroma to fill my dreams – Each day is full of growing – like the rose there is a life force of energy that empowers all of life – We become what we were created to be – Grace energizes that life force that moves us to dance over the Bridge of Our Becoming, share the loving cup and celebrate with all the hope that makes smooth those Uneven Edges –

For today twinkle and be jubilant – Yes!

Contents

The Bridge 1
Uneven Edges 3
Petticoat Waves 4
Ribbons 6
Hail, Goliath 7
The Phenomenon 8
Killer Words 9
A Flower 10
No Lavender in My Life 13
Daffodils 14
The Far Shore 15
A Rainbow of Reality 16
A Journey 19
Sunflowers 20
Deny Clutter / Allow Life 23
The Gift 24
Dancing 26
A Sea Find 27
Paper Whites for a New Year 28
A Visit 29
One Valentine's Fate 31
Sanctuary Days 32
On the Walk 33
Rays of Wonder 34
The Mysterious Mistake 36
More Uneven Edges 39
What a Choice 40
This Storm Ends 41
Old Friends 43
The Red Door 45
Breath - A Rolling Thought 46
The Seagulls' Meeting I See Silver 47
I See Silver 47
Moving Day: What's in the Other Room? 48
Balloon Man 49
Why Things Are Like They Are 50
My Aunt Annie 52
Endurance 53
The Morning Walker 55
Life's Daisy Chain of Days 56
Aunt Annie's Candy Jar 57
Never Force a Fit 58

Messages on the Wind 60
Twinkle from Your Heart 61
The Empty Space 63
A Brotherly Dispute 64
Our God Moment 66
Dearly Departed 68
Respect and Joy 69
Gypsy Flower Dance 71
Walk the Road 72
Round 74
An Easter Thought 77
Friendship 2001 78
Forever Friends 81
Soul Dance 82
Energy 84
The Embrace 86
The Choice the Heart Makes 87
Atlantis 88
The Quiet Hour 91
The Tide Within 92
The Parade 95
Grief 96
Songs of the Spirit 97
The Smile 99
A Journey 100
Get in the Path of Life 102
Be Faithful 104
A Joyful Heart 105
Passion 106
A Thought 107
Trap Doors 108
One Dance 109
Where Do We Put Our Lonely? 110
Sea Moments 111
The Day of the Dolphins 112
Imagination Tale 113
Leaving the Ball 114
Uneven Edges 115
It's a Sweet Life if You're Drinking from the Loving Cup 116
Jubilation Juice 117
Conclusion 118
Acknowledgments 119

The Bridge

In clock-time, our feet stand at the very center of the little bridge.
At the head of this span lies the foggy mist of our essence,
Swirling in God's love before He sends His children out to live.
We crawl and toddle and skip across the boards,
Falling often, sustaining splinters and little hurtful cuts.
Sometimes a helpful hand pulls us up.
Sometimes a bully shoves us down again.
As we stand astride the center point, we feel the broken parts
    rattle inside.
No one can see, but we know. We feel the truth.
At that exact moment, the breath of grace descends into our weary soul
And makes love fair shine like a crystal sun.
Our very self is gathered up and blessed forever.
Our steps to the end of the bridge are in sync with our mission
    and our marrow.
At bridge's end, we return to the space of endless time,
    having walked the Bridge of our Becoming.

Uneven Edges

There are greedy little gray thoughts abroad today
That twist and turn a little and turn good convictions downward.
Glib spin and moments held captive – on hold, on hold, on hold.
I have lost a year filling out repetitive forms that state only
  shadow surface statistics.
I have filled out a forest of papers for people who never read them
  but charge a fee.
Everyone asks questions and is offended when you do not tell them all.
They assume their right to know is righteous and just.
Like our flowing streams so clogged with pollutants, judgmental asides,
  greedy motives slip into the flow of our daily lives
And turn it gray with smug egos' oozings.
Hucksters loudly offer empty solutions to correct our flabby images.
Poor world, you have taken a beating, and people are sad.
I make a pledge to you to do just one thing a day to thank you
  for giving me a home, dear world.
The edges may always be uneven, but we can make smooth a
  resting place, a spot of beauty for our family of travelers.
A world where each journey is important, and no one is ever on hold . . . .
  on hold . . . . on hold . . . .

Petticoat Waves

In early morn, the waves sashay in like a maiden's petticoats
   afloat with quick small steps.
Curls of white foam bubble gently as they slide ashore.
The stub grass on the dunes clumps and digs into the sand.
As yet, no one, not even a bird, has cut the clear bright landscape.
The beginning of an ocean day . . . .
In the still quiet we think about how alive our passions flow.
As does the ocean floor, we have levels and depths.
Close to the shore we welcome many wading feet.
This is the frolicking area where we all play a lively game of tag.
The deeper the water the fewer companions toss in the tide with us.
There is an aloneness that captures us in the waves' curl.
We crest with the excitement of our deepening adventure.
Life roars through our bodies as the waves repeat their rhythmic cadence.
How alive we feel in the deep roll of the sea.
We have been cradled in a profound dimension for a few
   breathless moments.
Then, like water babies, we have been held up and playfully channeled
   back to shore.
This tingling jubilation of an embrace with the deep, deep water . . .
It seems we understand anew the texture of our souls.
Our inner tides in sync with the wonder and power of the sea
   Cause us to kneel in joyous thanksgiving.

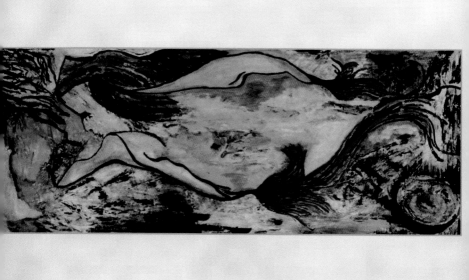

Ribbons

I remember ribbons of every color flowing from the rafters of my
    canopied bed.
Through the open window the fog flew in, sliding like a dove among the
    rainbow of ribbons.
The fog moistened my pillow with a cold freshness.
A gypsy tambourine hung on the bedpost, the bells shivering in dawn's first
    foggy breath.
Clutching covers, I watched and listened.
A mysterious moment, perhaps the ending of a dream . . .
Perhaps the beginnings of a day arriving to intrigue this child to life's bold
    adventure.
My dreams have always been tied with bright colored ribbons.
The music of my life has the punch of gypsy tambourines.
In this night's silence, a memory remains of fog, flowing ribbons,
    and the far-off sound of bells calling this little girl.

Hail, Goliath

Science grows like Goliath to an unnatural size,
Prodding and poking our every fiber in the name of good,
Siphoning off bits of our essence for profit or curiosity.
We are becoming our own invasions of aliens,
As they try to capture and possess the uniqueness of our very genes.
When science is consumed with greed and pride
It grows twisted and poisonous with mutants.
The wounded need a healer, very wise and humble when touching life.
The bankrupt life hungers for a way to be whole again.
We long for a springtime of innocence and fresh growth.
We yearn to sing a song that can be heard over the music.
We hunger for the gentle feather-touch of love.
We must insist the soul be inviolate even under Goliath's siege.

The Phenomenon

Streaking across the night sky, white, luminous like a flash
They appear from nowhere, like a chord of music from a silent pool.
Sucked into the dark sky, this elegant growing presence
What is this breathtaking wonder?
So many now come dancing through the sky.
Have I happened upon angels dancing a magical minuet?
Perhaps the stars are rearranging their universal order to secretly catch
    us unawares.
The night sky is playing a silent symphony that draws the mind into
    eternal time.
Now appears the barest outline of a white seabird wing,
Criss-crossing the sky like a glowing rocket landing in the darkest tunnel
    in the sky,
Very like arrows shooting from earth to heaven.
The eternal music in my heart longs to join the white, white seabird
    and pierce the darkness to find and to reflect the light that wraps
    my heart and my soul
And see beyond this present vale.

Killer Words

If you love me, be kind – your gentle words of caring emit an aura of
  precious love.
Those words that cut, offered up with ego and control, can never be
  forgotten.
Can *never* be forgotten.
Beware – use your power wisely.
There is no way to erase words spoken in cowardly self glory,
  piercing another's dignity.
Only humble words, those small words of respect, receive the blessing that
  gives life to love.

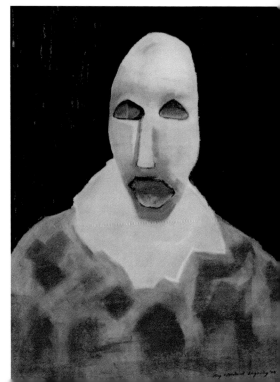

A Flower

When you meet a lady, sir, always have a flower in your hand
   or planted in your heart.
There is always a nervous, lonely spot to be soothed, you see.
A twig of jasmine for her hair or a nosegay for her pillow.
A gentle smile and eyes that fix firm in her direction.
A touch upon her elbow to guide her down the stair . . . .
Be aware, gentle man, that a flower is the perfect word to Bless
   the lady's day.

No Lavender in My Life

Lavender – the scent is full of soft closeness.
The color seems drained of life.
It is a measly shadow of the royal purple,
Lacks the seductive passion of aubergine,
Is lost next to the romance of the lover's lilac.
Like velvet, silk and taffeta, each has a flow and a style.
The lavender calico has been used, washed, worn thin.
No, no, I will not ride the silver train nor eat the shining golden apple
  wearing pale lavender.
And yet, in my garden, I gather gentle lavender and tie it with a ribbon
  in my hair.
Perhaps we do treasure the delicate wisdom that quietly surrounds life
  with a subtle beauty that pleasures our aging days.
We remember the dancing taffeta of aubergine, the silky lilac gown on that
  romantic evening, the purple velvet of those strong and strutting years.
But, lo, I think now that the softness of the lavender gown
  will indeed comfort my time abed.
I giggle a bit about these lavender moments and silly wanderings.
Good-bye.

Daffodils

Don't sing just the sad songs, my friend.
Seek out the first daffodil of spring,
Still dusted with March snow.
The precious tingling feeling inside,
The knowing that the parade of treasures will soon begin.
The hyacinths, the tulips, the sweet, sweet lilac . . .
I always wonder whether 'tis fair
To pick that first daffodil for my pleasure
Or leave it there to welcome the coming parade.

The Far Shore

Like the ocean depths hiding secret
shelves of life
My soul tumbles through territories
unknown
Sliding through the shining water to know
what lies ahead
Stopping beneath a covered shell to side
step a danger in my path
Resting between the coral buds to grow
and gather strength -
Each moment is alive with the
currents of life in and around me
If you are very still, you can hear the
heartbeat of eternity -
For our heartbeat is an echo of all
the living on the earth -
As we somersault through our days,
we risk and we grow
So revel in the moments and
the wonders of the journey
'Tis our creative essence that floats with
the tide to our eternal homeland's shore.

A Rainbow of Reality

On the dresser there is powder and paint in a rainbow of colors.
Taking the brush, the lady begins to imagine her reality.
Color for her lips, cheeks and eyes, she feels the picture surfacing.
Subtly, she shades the curve of the cheek, the upturn of her lip.
A smile filters along her profile as she exits home.
She turns to face the passerby with expectations of a nod of recognition.
Her aliveness grows, as others respond to her cordial manner.
The lady dares to share a dream with a listener.
What power the listener possesses for the reality of both their worlds!
This striving to span from soul to soul walks a fragile bridge over a
    canvas of loneliness.
There is a deep yearning to touch the reality of another.
In twin-like trust for a moment, the magical mix bears joyful affirmation,
    and there is a rainbow in her heart.

A Journey

The falcon soared, plunged, and cut the air cleanly with each turn.

A brush from the old hemlock plucked a feather from the mighty wing.

Unnoticed, the falcon swooped down upon his prey; he rose skyward, a
  victor from his hunt.

A breeze caught the belly of the proud feather, wafting to an earthbound
  rock.

The wind made music swirling through the canyon walls,

And from a cave a spring slashed down the mountainside, carrying
  the cascading feather to the valley floor.

A noble feather resting in the reeds dried quickly in the hot sun.

The mighty eagle keenly chose this treasure for her nest on high.

It is so painful never to be near the sky – in the gathering of sticks
  and stones that build our lives.

Let us handle with awe that feather, that treasured work of art
  that soared on falcon wings and caught the living winds of time.

Like the great eagle, remember to look up and glide.

Sunflowers

Someone brought me sunflowers early on a Saturday morning.
The summer was very strong and heat went through your hat.
Suddenly the day became extraordinary, as if the flowers
  warmed the inside of me.
The big-hearted flower shed golden dust and caused me to sit still,
  smile, even laugh out loud.
A friend bringing sunflowers does indeed make for an extraordinary day.

Deny Clutter / Allow Life

Clutter fills our houses, our lives, our minds.
We are bulging with stuff to the popping point.
We are Velcro-ed from head to toe with bits of sales graffiti;
We are an easy sell, always hoping to be more beautiful, think smarter,
    or live in the perfect McMansion.
As we sit amid this array of goods we knew we had to have
Tears fall from nowhere and we feel suffocated and bewildered.
Life cannot flourish, be creative or move amid all these
    attention grabbers and upkeep cloggers.
Let us shed the layers and enjoy roaming room and quiet spots
    of beauty to inspire and create.
Let the sighs of our life echo and vibrate –
Let us dance thru our halls, draw pictures on the walls,
Laugh and twinkle and dazzle our mind and heart.

The Gift

God's greatest gift is trusting us with children –
To smile into their first smile
To see our child cradle her blessed child.
In between lies the beautiful and terrifying growing time;
Those uneven edges – the giving, the taking, the letting go –
Our learning is not without pain.
God's love is perfect; each life given is a life unique.
Both mother and child have a destiny to fulfill.
To understand – there is a golden thread that balances
    this precious blessing –
It is the raw edge of honoring with love and forgiveness
    all of our human imperfections.
Deep streams of humility and compassion make sweet that steady love
    that breaks the chains of earthly wrongs.
God's light opens the flower in our heart
And we bloom eternally, brilliantly and joyfully.

Dancing

Cold and dripping, the glisten slides downward.
Nature sheds her frozen face.
Washed anew, the trees behold the January day.
The forest trees are bare, looking like slender ballerinas on point,
Just holding until the music starts.
I, too, hold my breath, anticipating new thoughts to appear as
guideposts for my day.
There is time today to sort among my thoughts
And melt away the hardened attitudes that have stuck to my days.
So I stretch all my being on point, awaiting that special music
that is mine alone to dance.

A Sea Find

Bobbing like corks between the breakers,
A gathering of gulls floats peacefully, sharing the moment,
Balanced and secure among the swells.
The tide deposits a billow full of shells: some broken, some quite ordinary.
Perhaps one is a treasure from the sea.
One shell is riddled with the life struggle of the one who lived within.
Somehow the holes and chiseled lines seem more precious than the
unblemished gift.
The invisible undercurrents that push and pull at our marrow surface,
leaving their mark.
Some may smoothly cover time's etchings;
Others weave their adventures into their souls
And bob like corks between the breakers.

Paper Whites for a New Year

Buried deep under the rocks, life begins to stir.

The cool and gentle water trickles down to the bulb lying among the
pebbles.

Unlocked to live, the green shoots almost spring to the surface to seek the
sun.

More water – more shoots . . .

More water – taller and taller . . .

More water – a bud appears!

It almost makes you laugh to see how fast life seeks to live.

Then, oh, on the first day of this New Year, the aroma of paper whites
filled my morning air.

The delicate white blooms were the beauty of life born anew.

The blossoms of promise herald the hope I seek in all my days to come.

Paper whites – a New Year. . .

The promise is alive.

A Visit

Oh, it's just me – I need to come in and
join you
To sit together as children do, sharing patches of our thoughts
We can take a peek at the longings in our heart
It's good to be with you – you listen closely
with care in your heart –
Our talk is weightless as if gliding
on soft wings of total understanding
I've noticed you always wait expectantly
for me
And I come more often now because I know
where you are –
This exquisite visit washes the soul
comforts the spirit, and causes the heart
to shine.

One Valentine's Fate

Love expressed and dared to be sent on Valentine's Day –
A feeling escaping from a very shy heart
Tossed quickly on a breeze of hope,
Tingling anticipation awaiting that echo of mutual longing.
A beautiful afternoon of dreamtime.
Lo, night fell; only silence and the shining moon, but no returning breeze.

Sanctuary Days

Oh how I treasure those Sanctuary Days
They come between Christmas and New Year-
That time that is so private and quiet
That time that belongs to no one but you
To smile and lie on the bed, close your
eyes and slide from dream to dream-
A time for gumdrops and sweet oranges
A time to talk to God about hopes and
cry warm tears for the lost
I can become small in my sanctuary
chair and feel the largeness of all
about me-
To know that creation is a wonder
huge - all encompassing and eternal
the miracle is - I was given sanctuary.

On the Walk

The invisible breeze turned the basket fern just enough to kiss the sun.
The stepping stones ended at the forest door.
One could barely see a wild rambling rose cascade into the shadow
Pulling our soul into home of hemlock hedge, weeping fir and soft spruce,
    nestling close,
A panoply of greenery still shining from the rain
Smelled of pine; one could almost feel the breath of the woodland.
So still this world of nature, hiding the power of the tall trees.
I go walking there with all the raging passions in my soul,
And somehow their power turns my heart just enough to kiss the sun.

Rays of Wonder

The brilliance of the light that afternoon empowered the windows
   to shine as if alive,
The aisle of the cathedral awash with a celestial rainbow.
I stood captured in a prism of unspeakable beauty.
Every color fair glistened, gathering my spirit to dance and soar with joy.
The light of heavenly graciousness shone into my heart
To warm the love that makes home there.
And my spirit burst forth with rays of wonder
So I could share my essence with other souls nearby.

The Mysterious Mistake

Oh, yes, my friend, the choice does count:
To go this way with one or that way with another.
It may be a bother to choose, but not to select is to go wrong.
To keep a soul we must feed it with real direction,
Not cling to the coattail of a fast-talking huckster.
When you follow the music into the alley
Be prepared for the darkness lurking there.
Be bold with your fears and cover them with grace.
Letting go lightens the pace and makes the direction truer.
The mysterious and eternal mistake is *not* to make the choice.

More Uneven Edges

Today was one of those fluffy cloud days –
A bit like whipped cream in Grand's blue ironstone bowl.
It was delicate April filled with cherry blossoms and fragile sweet peas.
Spring is here and as welcome as a childhood friend.
The air was perfumed with lilac and the breeze gentle through her hair.
The Lady at the gate waited expectantly, her very breath a little rushed.
She lingered, looking longingly down the path.
As she leaned forward to pick the nearby daffodil, a tear
    slipped down her cheek.
She tucked her precious dream deep into her imagination.
For today no one will hear the music in her heart or see her eternal shadow.

What a Choice

We must jump into life as if it were a great and grand pile of
   autumn leaves –
A pile of many shapes, many colors, many sizes, no two alike.
Shall we frolic in the great beautiful mosaic?
Or shall we try to bag them up by Wednesday, trash day?
The choice is yours. As often said,
"Have a nice day."

This Storm Ends

After the storm, the waves touch shore
with a gentle swish as if to soothe
away the pounding of the angry
waters–
Life's anger whips and blows and rattles the day-
Passes on hurt and confusion and broken spirits-
Like the musical instrument we must
retune
So that we share a melody gentle to the senses
If we listen with awareness, we become part of the sounds,
We become like the wave slipping
into shore bringing offerings
of shells to delight the little ones.

Old Friends

As the waves make their wet inevitable landing,
The sand heaves and gulps the water like a thirsty dragon.
The waves speak in crashing little hiccups,
Pushed down the wide corridor by a strong and willful wind.
The nimble sea oats wave to the pelicans floating by.
The sand and the wind and the water are ancient and eternal friends.
Wind pushing water, water moving sand, always touching, always alive.
Never resting as they change the world –
Each gives, each yields.
We hardly notice this powerful triad.

Kay Woodard Lagerberg

The Red Door

As I awoke, the sun, fair red, rose on a golden cord.
It sat in the sky like a shining red doorway,
Open for a moment for us to enter the other side of creation.
Then, quickly rising to hide its magical pathway,
Took its seat high on the horizon of the sea.
We three stood watching, marveling at the secret we then knew.
Dawn is the special moment to sail beyond this world
And greet the world that lies beyond –
A place that belief whispers is truly there,
A home we know through prayer.

Breath –
A Rolling Thought

Breath of God – my breath – deep breath – clean air –
fragrance in the air – air renewing my being - the Air of Life –
the higher – the thinner – the colder

Breath gives us the strength to go on – Our breath carries
our words – moves us – Breathing is the first thing and the last
thing that we do – sigh – gasp – deep – halting – rapid – peaceful
– so expressive of who we are – fuels our brains and blows out the
candles on the cake

The Seagulls' Meeting

Down by the sea on a bluebird day,
Seven seagulls met to pray.
They rode the waves in a tight little bunch
As if they all gathered there to "do lunch."
They rested and floated, a funny sight to see,
Not unlike my friends and me!

I See Silver

Little slivers of silver crown the cresting wave
   that glides gracefully into shore.
The rhythmic cadence captures the weary spirit.
Its hushed song draws us as the Lorelei into its spell.
Content to be with the mysterious and majestic creation, we receive
   a gift, which echoes in our hearts for a lifetime.

Moving Day: What's in the Other Room?

———◆———

As we left the ole homestead on that cold and rainy day,
We walked hand in hand, saying our goodbyes to those rooms where life
    was daily lived:
The bedroom where generations were born and where the sun came first dawn,
The nursery and the children's room chipped from flying toys and
    crayoned pictures left on closet doors,
A kite still hanging from the ceiling waiting for a windy day.
The attic stairs creaked one last time as we pulled the old cedar chest down
    to the front hall.
We touched the soft and silky banister that supported generations of climbers
    and descenders.
In the parlor there were a few needles from the Christmas tree pushed into
    the corner, and stocking nails still hung in the mantle wood.
The dining room seemed so empty without all those who had come and shared
    table and company.
I can see the old poinsettia withering on the porch.
Last and best-loved, the kitchen, the heart of the home . . .
You can still smell the bread and feel the laughter and tears of love.
Out that back door which welcomed all life that came here. . .
Now we go to another room, an ancient room of wonder where we can live
    the mystery of all time to come.
Prepare. . . .

Balloon Man

Come, Mr. Balloon Man.
I will fill each happy colored ball with all manner of secret messages,
And let them float 'til they land I know not where.
Shower thoughts in foreign lands to unknown souls living there.
They would be filled with such as this, I think:
The memory of a little touch of kindness,
The thought of love shared extravagantly,
An important truth that I must savor,
The unexpected glimpse of healing beauty,
A laugh and a smile, those twins of delight,
A loving touch that assures someone is there.
Yes, fill all the dancing colors with good tidings, and let them soar,
For we must look up and fill the atmosphere with friendly things.
Welcome the Easter sky with a grateful heart and a joy that sweetly rings
As our souls dance toward heaven in a rainbow of silent balloons.

Why Things Are Like They Are

———— ❖ ————

As the rhythm of the seas flows ashore, it stirs an echo in the heart.
Microchips of memory provide verse to creative solitudes, urging refrains.
Life echoes in a hundred-voice choir within the depths of quiet solitude.
Decisions of today play tag with memories of decades ago.
The image of the little girl folds into the mother, the grandmother, the
    patterns chosen for me today.
Be it harshly critical or gently secure, each action springs from ancient
    origins.
The dance has been continuous, but the rhythm has changed at will.
Oh, creative soul, gather all the ages in the amphitheater, all the memories
    march forth.
Drink them all and stir your creative spirit.
Dance your life aloud and add your music to the echoes of the ages.

Kay Woodard Lazenby '62

My Aunt Annie

As she sat soaking in the splendor of the sunset
Her face was so warmly aglow that you could almost see her dream.
Her appearance was soft with the thoughts that scribbled lines upon her
brow.
Her deep desires and longing left a kindness in her smile and true pleasure
in her laugh.
The wisdom of her ninety years is a blessing, and the light from her eyes
reassures and comforts the doubting heart.
She reveals real life; indeed our imaginations can see the outline of a soul.
I am transported through the invisible to a larger place.
A memory eternal is inscribed in both of our hearts.
We have filled a few moments with very special love.

Endurance

As I turned the corner, I saw her about five feet ahead;
Her gait was slow and she leaned a little to the right.
Her shape was full, with shoulders that willed her forward.
It wasn't long before my stride and pace passed her slowing gait.
I stopped to look into a window, but in reality I was compelled
   to look at the unremarkable passenger coming closer.
To my surprise, her eyes were alive and very aware,
And when our eyes met she smiled for a moment and then
   concentrated on her journey.
My thoughts flashed. This dear lady has endured and you somehow
   knew she would continue to endure.
In this random moment I received an unexpected gift:
Those who endure bless us with a quiet assurance that a small life can be
   of great worth.
It was as if my tea was sweetened with precious honey
And a great lady had passed by.

The Morning Walker

As I moved down the street on that spring morning
The crispness of the air filled my lungs with a tingle of renewal.
The pear trees danced in the breeze like dancers atwitter
 before the music starts.
A gentleman is approaching; he moves in sync with his daily routine:
His shoulders a little stooped, his hair thick and white, his statue lean;
 and moving with a kindness and grace.
My eyes noticed his slender fingers carefully holding six large and
 sunny daffodils.
I felt the great desire to know who would receive this thoughtful bouquet –
Perhaps a granddaughter would be coming for an afternoon visit
 and they would be her gift.
Maybe his mate of many years would smile at the shared love between them.
It could be that the daffodils would be placed on his kitchen table
 to keep him company at breakfast time.
No matter what their fate, I delight in silently passing this gentle soul
 with his special gift of beauty.
He shared unknowingly his treasure and its goodness with this stranger.

Life's Daisy Chain
of Days

Some days, the dewy drops of doubt crowd our every thought.
Smooth waters can be churned quickly when monster hurts
   break the surface.
Locks and dams flood the peaceful landscape of our life.
Negative winds and a hurricane of fear turn us weak.
As quickly, our inner eye seeks the harmony and the beauty
   that is also our reality.
The children, the flowers, the music, the friends –
The years of droplets of goodness.
Our doubts remember children's hugs, our hearts are full
   of love scattered along our daisy chain.
Life's adventure pushes us ever forward to gather one flower
   for this day lived whether ill or good.
For the living of a real life takes courage and faith,
The result a chain of real moments – so simple, so blessed, so rare.

Aunt Annie's
Candy Jar

The children never knew what sugary goodie was in the candy jar.
The jar had multicolored roses on the top; alas! there was a
    small chip in the yellow rose.
An eager little hand had rushed to find a treat and bruised the rose.
Jelly beans or gumdrops, King Leo sticks red, green, yellow,
Orange slices, candy corn and kisses wrapped in foil,
Homemade peanut brittle, hard candy of every color,
Life Savers, licorice sticks and everyone's favorite, Tootsie Rolls!
The candy treat was oh, so good, as was Aunt Annie's pat
    and stories of old.
There was laughter. 'Twas the happiest corner of the world –
Sweet candy and a heartfelt hug.

Never Force a Fit

As we wander over ideas and under actions,
We travel around objections and between conflict,
Side-stepping consequences
All the while burdened by excuses.
Where is the fit? How does it all flow together?
A peg cannot be shoved or pushed into the wrong space;
A fit has to be perceived and guided by real choices.
The carpentry work of life may meander like the river,
But, like the river, all flow must slip into the eternal fit –
Beauty – Love – Peace
The perfect fit is never, never random.

Messages on the Wind

Oh, yes, the day is dark.
The wind carries the dust of soldiers' marching boots.
It is wind that carries sparks of fire from tree to tree,
    becoming an inferno.
The dark funnel tornado carries rooftops and trees
    down the countryside.
Oh, wind, you toss the big boats like corks upon the waves.
The camels lie behind the dunes as sand fills the air in a blinding rage.
Lo, there is a kinder side to this unseen power:
A gentle breeze cools us on a summer day;
In little puffs the kite is carried aloft behind running children
    squealing with delight.
This invisible wind touches and changes all of life, high and low.
Raging and ebbing as it swirls from cloud to forest to sea,
It changes the world with whipping fury.
And yet on tiptoe as quietly as the gliding moon
It carries the aroma of rose and lilac and Confederate jasmine.
What a mystery, the life of this unseen power, be it
Raging like the dragon or hushed whispers in the night.
This creation, most unique, this phantom of the skies.

Twinkle from Your Heart

As life walks us higher and higher up the mountain
Things change...the grade becomes steeper and often we need a hand to
steady us or give us a little tug up –
Often we have to pause to rest.
When we look about, the air is clear and we can see the long trail below that
we have mastered –
The wood flowers we have picked, the merry streams we have splashed through,
the uneven, rocky paths where we have struggled to keep our balance.
We see the valley below...the place of our beginnings when we came together
on this life's path.
We are a band of travelers sharing this mysterious climb to the mountain top.
Now that we are almost there, something magic has happened.
We stop and look at the beautiful place where we have arrived.
Our view is so very clear.
All of a sudden, little twinkles of light and love beam from each heart,
Sheer joy lights this moment of twinkling hearts and showers down on those in
the valley whose journey has just begun.

So, my friends, embrace the life of now and share your twinkle, yes your twinkle
from the heart.

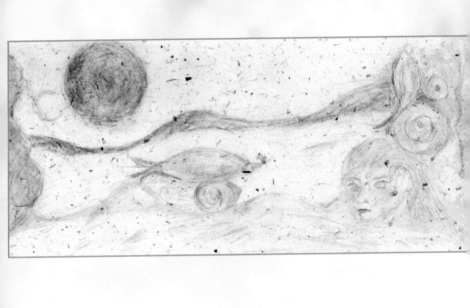

The Empty Space

As day breaks, I am roused: the future is here.

But, lo! something is very, very wrong.

All of the people and familiar places are gone.

Everything had seemed all right, but sleep had come with restless flutters;

A feeling of loss had hovered near for some days past.

Before me lies the empty space, spread like a huge lake on the horizon.

No boat at hand, no bridge across, too far to swim to the other shore.

I am lost in my empty space.

Others are going to and fro and seem not to be in emptiness at all.

As I sat, bewildered, the waves lapped at my feet, swishing and washing
   away the worldly crustiness that had covered my attention.

Slipping further into the waters, shoulder high, a gentle letting go freed my
   feelings of loss.

I went deeper under the welcoming waves, unafraid.

Slowly rising to the surface, I am on the other shore.

Rested, I felt my spirit sing and my heart eager to share.

I will come often to this Lake of the Lord

To wash away the dust of doubts,

To fill the empty space with the spirit of rest and love and joy!

A Brotherly Dispute

Big Brother had made ten trips to the well,
The buckets all filled and safely on the porch.
Little Brother sat with his dipper on the end of the step,
Dipping and spilling ladles full of water, making slippery mud puddles.
Anger gripped Big Brother. A heartfelt sock knocked the little fellow
clean off his step,
Followed by a tooth-loosener of a whack.
Mama came upon this screaming scene.
She grabbed Big Brother, her paddle swinging hard and fast.
Justice, oh justice. Are you sure?

Our God Moment

Are we not all searching with inner passion to find our God moment?
It is almost a desperate need to know, to possess, to be really sure
That truth is truth and our spirit is safe.
Our every fiber wants to emit assurance.
We must not fail to cling to God.
In reality, it is God that holds us with tender love.
In those times when shameful doubts pinch at our truth,
When differences rouse hurts and
Batter our calm and good intentions,
Trust, yes trust, holds our hand
'Til the light comes
And assures us that our moment is eternal.

Dearly Departed

Through and in death shines life.
Those that leave us leave their dust,
Their essence upon our heart.
This uneven edge of loss casts us into a tornado of feelings.
When there are two, time seems friendly and full.
One is one, and never more than one.
But the memory can unfold shared times that have enriched
  our days and make us more than one.
We carry in our life album those who have journeyed with us.
We have sung songs, danced, laughed, even wept,
And held each other tight.
Our heart never loses the beat of life we shared
Nor the eternity that will join us forever.

Respect and Joy

Respect is a dapper gentleman
Bowing deep to show care for all those present.
The small girl stood tall and wore gingham
With a noticeable elegant air.
She came with great expectations, waiting to be expressed.
She walked into the silence, unsure, but feeling great wonder.
This was her moment of bravery;
This was her first holy moment.
She smiled, she threw her arms full wide –
She danced and danced through the crowd
    to tell us of her joy.
She was met with deep bows of respect
And desires to be her partner and her friend.

Gypsy Flower Dance

As the moon rose, full and silver,
Streams of light fell upon the hidden forest.
There was an eerie mist floating among the pines.
Strange callings from the owl,
A moaning howl from the mother wolf.
There was no wind. Stillness froze the world.
A sudden gust of wind enlivened that mysterious place.
Instantly, the gypsy flowers that covered the forest floor
Began to dance a wild and swirling tarentella.
They danced with total abandon.
Their colors ran together, making a rainbow under the radiant moon.
What had been quiet and peaceful
Became a crashing symphony of dancing color –
A never-before-seen ritual.
These rare gypsy roses celebrated the beauty of the magical moon –
Suddenly gone into the wayward wind, just a flicker of gypsy roses
Kissing a princess moon.

Walk the Road

She knew the road well for she had felt each stone underfoot.
She had paused under the shade tree when the sun was hot.
She picked the snowy Queen Anne's lace that drifted down the slope.
Yes, she knew the road she walked and the people who lived behind
closed doors, in houses along the way.
The narrow road has a well-trod path with little offshoots to
the low thicket patch of briars.
She doesn't go there except at blackberry time, and with great care
lest there be a rattler living there.
The seasons change from wild red poppies to black-eyed Susans smiling,
then the sticky burrs and nuts of fall, and at last the Christmas
holly berry.
She has spent a lifetime upon this path to the small town and back to her
one room: one room and a porch.
She walks this road where life is exploding.
The traps are ever near to catch those unaware,
But also purple velvet pansies to welcome a lonely morning walk.
The beauty of the woodland path encircles her as she walks, and the sun
warms her cheek.
She truly lives and walks the path with heart, but she walks alone.

Round

I have found
Everything is round.
From the mulberry bush that we all know
To Dorothy's tornado that scooped her up with Toto.
In the universe, many numbers and shapes are found,
But we were given a little world that was perfectly round.
Even Santa's pipe blows little round rings
And apple pie is one of life's marvelous things!
Rings are round on our marriage day,
And merry-go-rounds where happy children play.
As I tie a yellow ribbon 'round the old oak tree
All other shapes seem impossible to me –
Triangles, hexagons, parallelograms are all sound,
But please give me a good ole circle that's perfectly round!

An Easter Thought

You placed a shawl of love around my shoulders

And covered my sins with a cloth of purity.

You spread a rug of support for my knees to fall upon;

You covered me with the blanket of true forgiveness;

You have woven me into your family tapestry.

My blessings are boundless for I am draped eternally in your Easter Love.

Friendship 2001

It is in our collectiveness that a part
of our individuality is born
It is in our own unique individuality
that our friendship flourishes
It is our friendship that makes our
collectiveness become unique
This lovely mystery has blended our
hearts over the years
Today we rejoice for we all have Today!

Kay Woodland Lazenby

Forever Friends

For these many years our journeys have been intertwined.

We have walked our own paths but always come together to break bread
and share the day.

We have built a forever blessed bond of friendship.

First, love – we forever love and are loved.

Next, strength – in every trial or difficulty we give and receive strength,
one to another.

We understand and care and do not tire of listening.

We stand with each other.

We have been taught from above what *I will never leave thee or forsake thee*
means.

It is good to share this journey, to laugh and celebrate with an amazing,
merry heart all the years we have been given.

And so we celebrate together today and all the tomorrows,
for we are forever friends.

We begin our solitary dance knowing not the steps
   but having all the feelings
The enormity of being alive takes a lifetime
   of moving along our own growing horizon line
Our music flows from the soul – our eternal living being.
The steps are taught and danced to this world's demanding rhythm
Time layers many raggedy coats upon us to slow our dance.
The struggle to slip free from these rags of worldliness,
   the pattern of our daily life.
We ache to fill our incompleteness
   with the Holy light of eternal Blessing.
Our inner rhythm, like the moonlit tides,
Is in harmony and balance with our Eternal Holy Purpose.
The arch of love is our Bridge
Let us seek our time to dance with enormous jubilation
Ere eternity envelopes our soul.

Energy

Each world wanderer travels with his own energy mystic.
Our own first burst of life is a push, a slap and a resounding cry of being!
Every impulse is energized by the silent will to live joyously.
Upon seeing his own image, the baby laughs,
    and thus begins that feeling of well-being that laughter bestows.
The loving touch of mother ignites the energy to reach out and meet life.
The romping child has boundless energy to seek every wonder of day and night.
Friendship energizes two to explore and share the beauty of the world –
Love encourages our deepest longings to unite,
    creating a force of life that grows, renews and fills the emptiness.
Our Lord holds our essence, our energy, in His hands –
He loves, protects, expands our very being
    to energize eternity and add life to the universe.

The Embrace

The pain of loss gives way to a feeling of desperation and deep loneliness.
A large piece of our being has cracked and disappeared into the land of
never.
A great abyss of emptiness stares back at us.

This new space – now a part of my spirit and daily life.
This loss can turn a life filled with traditional behavior into frightening
    nothingness.

The struggle that follows is Act Two, a necessary battle to understand the
coming of Act Three.
The space within gives new seeds a place to grow –
The ground has been plowed by loss.

The Struggle has been New Choices –
The Victory is the accepting Embrace of our loving creator.
In wholeness, our inner spirit is at peace
And our outer spirit can meet life with our own loving embrace.
No hole in the heart – just a locket of memories and loving keepsakes.

The Choice
the Heart Makes

Daily life, made of seconds and minutes,
Shrinks and expands with our own breath –
Small, immediate chores, enormous life commitments placed in our daily
hours.
We sort out, make choices to direct our days –
Each love-wrapped choice inspired, blessed and empowered
As if a giant loom wove the myriad threads into the portrait of our life –
A harmony of pattern and color reveals our spirit caught in action.
Our breath – the very texture of our spirit – gives our heart the power to
make love visible.
Let your giving tumble freely, making music
Mighty music as you live this beautiful eternal journey.

Atlantis

Along some foreign shore, Atlantis rises from the deep.
At first dawn's blush, color streaks along the horizon line.
'Tis magic to catch this rare sight –
Atlantis rises today on the shore to gulp the air
   and sigh with longing never to touch this world.
There's just enough light to see this ancient metropolis.

Suddenly, the mysterious Atlantis sinks deep,
   to float along the ages.
How extraordinary to glimpse this secret glory of ages past!
This day will forever be golden in memory.

The Quiet Hour

When the moment is quiet and very still
We sit, almost smiling, washing our memories so they remain clear –
Letting our soul have a time to visit our heart,
Giving our innocence time to come out of hiding
    and romp with the reality of our faith,
Breathing deep, feeling that reality of God's strength at our elbow.

A holy time of thanksgiving
A searching time for wisdom
A peaceful time of assurance

We leave these silent moments and blow kisses to our children,
Laugh just because glee springs from our heart
And for a moment know the blessing of life's wonder.

The Tide Within

Low gray waves swished at dawn – gentle, soft, warm –
So inviting, our beginnings of innocence and yieldedness.
A sweet coming to ourselves in protective arms.
As we walk the world's many beaches
    and face incoming tides
The pace of life quickens –
Some tides roar and push us into swirling eddies.
Others cradle our bodies and place us on friendly shores.

It is good to find a spot to be
    and not roam the sands of world and time.
Looking up, the white sea bird circles and circles.
We have looked up and found assurance;
We are caressed by the faithful rhythm of the sea
We are in sync with the eternal tides of time.

The Parade

Oh, what excitement! The parade is passing now!
Its route - I do not know from whence it came nor where its end.
The bands are many, loud, and moving fast;
The tuba um-pahs – the drums tap and beat.
All walk in sync and fill the air with celebration sounds.

The excitement lifts my spirits and I am drawn to join the revelers
    and be a part –
Some still standing on the side . . . watching.
I am pulled into this unexpected moving celebration.
The music and dancing feet enclose my spirit with exploding glee –
Don't fail to live . . . join in the parade that marches through your heart!

Grief

It is in our grief that we can learn to let go –
It is in the deep silence of feeling our losses,
In the sadness of shattered commitments that we seek to hear
   the prelude of hope -
That those paralyzed feelings will be softened
   and begin to meet life.
As we wade through those uneven edges of grief, we are called
   to answer the unknown with faith.
We *can* trust that renewal, the new spring washing over that vast unknown.
In allowing our grief, our letting go has been showered with the strength
   to welcome new life –
The barren season has been a growing edge –
Now, in the spring those blooming days are our blessing
And our peaceful heart is our reward.

Songs of the Spirit

There is a fluttering of wings in the heart and spirit
   when a baby is born.
When a child sees her first rose and smells its sweet aroma –
When lovers' eyes silently hold tight
   and there is music without words –
When a loved one walks the high cliff of death –
When faith turns the lock and the light of eternal love shines all around.
When we see how high the eagle can soar – no earthbound spirit he!
What lessons we learn when the flowers bloom and the tree bears fruit,
Nightingales sing and the dolphin smiles –
When friends linger and talk and laugh and share their dreams –
No illusion, these songs of the spirit,
Just an echo of the wings of our eternal future.

The Smile

When my babe knowingly looks into my eyes
And a smile flashes on that tiny face –
That beauty floods my whole being with the power of a shooting star.
Awesome, the explosion of love –
A momentary symphony of perfection
A hint of the shining edge of eternity.

A Journey

Be a calm stream, always flowing and alive -
Do not rush like the rapids, tossing spray in sundry directions.
Eternity is a long river that we travel,
   fulfilling our longing to experience the essence of the sights on the
   shores
And the power of the great moving waters that guide us.
The great river had a beginning long ago
When the shores melted and ran down the rocks to find the pool of its
   beginning.
Out of the humble heart comes wisdom,
Shared as we travel downstream
Gathering the riches from many shores.
One day our spirit, filled with the beauty of our living, slips quietly into the
   welcoming waters of eternity –
Our spirit celebrates the loving welcome
And the glorious opportunities of forever.

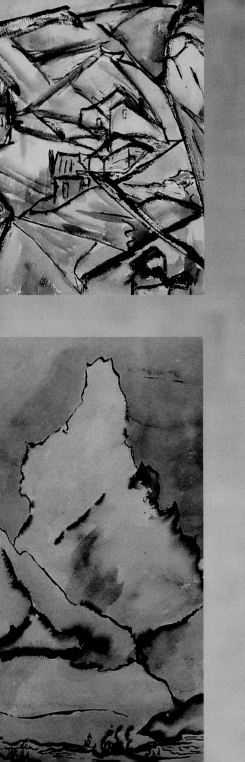

Get in the Path of Life

Whether you see life as a mountain, a road, a desert or an ocean
Choose to be in life's path.
Do not hide in a dark spot, becalmed and afraid.
If your spirit is that of a nomad, you may seek to keep your footing
    on the shifting, shifting sand,
Perhaps searching the horizon for the lush oasis' spring.
Seek and find the camel that is sure-footed and knows the hidden springs –
Mount his back to safely enter your journey across your eternal desert.
It may be the ocean deep that draws you into its rhythmic swaying waves
    and pulling tides.
The waves rise and ebb – there is no solid footing
No direction save the evening stars.
Climb into the boat that holds you safe,
Then journey across this amazing expanse of whale and turtle
    and polar bear –
Chart your course with the cap'n of your craft.
What an extraordinary life you will lead!
Perhaps life starts you on a city highway, all snarled with traffic and smog
    and loudly blowing horns and trucks that thunder by,
So overcome with the ever-pushing driving horde
That the way is not clear and panic makes you feel hopelessly lost.
Take your map and leave on exit three.
Breathe and reach the country road,
    so peaceful with ponds and cows, barns and fields of hay –

Treasure this space and the beauty of the land and the smiles and waves of
    passers-by.
Meeting life off exit three seems to give us time to be
    who we are meant to be.
Always keep your map in your pocket as you meet life on your road.
There are many mountains on the horizon, some high, some rugged
As we meet life and begin our climb.
The rocks are jagged and our footing slippery
But climb we must, driven by a spirit that directs our steps –
Holding tight to the rope that secures our every move.
Cold rock, narrow curving turns – still the spirit has no thought of turning
    back.
We do not know what is ahead
But we devote each muscle to holding us on course –
We are infused with strength to stay the course.

As if coming from a deep fog, we are at the mountain top –
The world below is so beautiful in the sunshine.
We have met life riding on our camel, sailing the deep waters in our boat,
    taking exit three on our map and, with our rope, reaching the
    mountain top of life.
Yes, meet life and walk your road
For you will receive the great gift you will need
And your spirit will be extraordinarily, eternally joyful!

Be Faithful

Be faithful – for it is the backbone of life's daily walk.
Absorb completely your commitment
To our Lord
To our family
To our friend
And to the needy along our path.
Let faithfulness run through your veins
And enliven every part of your living.
Understand the confused;
Laugh and turn a low time into joint pleasure.
Be silent and wait beside the lonely until fellowship bubbles through the
   loneliness.
Love deeply when a heart needs to be mended from worldly hurt.
Yes, as we stand in the cool waters of faithfulness we are buoyed up to hope.
We humbly accept each other and rejoice
That our hearts can love with such passion.

A Joyful Heart

Hearts should never be hidden for they are the gateway
  of every secret of our life:
The home of our emotions, our choices and our faith.
So often we lock down the chambers to hide pain, bitterness, suffered
  wrongs –
We clog the channels of our life flow.
We are so wonderfully made!
Our being sings like a full symphony with every member in full harmony.
The thrill of adding our music sets our heart in sync with what we are
  destined to be –
The pure in heart, the humble in heart, the generous in heart,
  the loving heart –
Oh, yes! There is nothing more beautiful than the beat of joy in the heart!

Passion

'Tis the gaiety of gratitude that moves our feet to dance –
Knowing all is well sponsors laughter even in the dark,
Seeing passion flow from the face of the old reflects promises fulfilled.
The gleeful singing of children at play reminds us of innocence's joy.
Be passionate, yes.
Let all be done with the passion that mirrors your heart's mighty purpose –
To be the child of eternity!

A Thought

Sitting in a pool of silence, yearning for wisdom –
A feeling of anticipation for what new song my heart will sing,
Knowing that the creativity of spirit will dance through the heart
    to unveil the path.
Remember when all was new and clean and innocent?
We look to see if there still remains Eden.
Lo, the garden still has the beauty of the rose, the butterfly, the bird –
If I can go with another whose heart can see the beauty, the wonder,
And remembers when all things were new and good –
Yes, my grandchild and I can walk together through that pool of silence
Delighting in the goodness and promise of what we share.

Trap Doors

When all seems balanced at last
And we are poised to watch the summer sun pour into the ocean
The trap door comes unhinged
And we plunge into the darkness of phones ringing and blaring music
    nearby,
Left only to imagine the beauty we had waited to see.

When all seems calm and at peace at last
And we are paused to lovingly share precious time with a loved one
The trap door gapes wide
And this precious time slips into work's demands and the buzz of text
    messages,
Leaving us saddened at the last hope of love quietly shared.

Time has glided on golden skates in and out of our dream time.
As we close our eyes, we breathe deeply
And an atmosphere of swirling faith lets us cross over those trap doors.
We open our eyes – we are on God's island of grace where all things are
possible.

One Dance

The rain trickled down the window pane, mocking the lady's tears.
Expectations slid away like the nightly autumn fog.
She had gone unnoticed even in her flowing gown;
Many gentlemen had passed her by on their way to dance.
As she turned to leave, a strong hand turned her elbow inward –
Their dance was like a magic dream that made her heart fair fly!
At midnight, all masks were taken off.
As she turned to know who made her heart dance,
She saw him slip into the night.
And the rain came down, as did her crystal tears.

Where Do We Put Our Lonely?

That fresh empty hole that aches –

We knew it when we were young and were the last chosen for Red Rover.

Somehow we did not exactly fit – an awkward feeling that hardened our
every muscle.

Small irregularities seemed so large as to be noticed.

There was so much beauty and spirit that was trapped, not knowing how to
become alive.

Separation – what a heartache that had no resuscitation – no breath to exhale
to a waiting world.

Our lonely hangs from our heart – beating - - beating --- beating – waiting to
be received.

In this breathless moment God's trumpet hails love's victory;

We no longer linger in our lonely.

No longer one but two.

We are free from the burden of solving everything.

We are free to love and care for those near us with enormous humility
and joy.

We breathe, we love, we are alive!

Sea Moments

The silver sleeves of first light warm the early tides of day.
The beach gulps the landing waves, scattering a treasure of shells abroad.
Ocean life has landed after years in moving waters.
The wind, the light, the tides and tiny shells – travelers all.
A moving mystery –
A secret of the eternal deep.

The Day of the Dolphins

Dawn poured rays of silver into the sea,
Etching the horizon like a silver frame.
It is the day of the dolphins!
Their fins sliced the sea ever so close to shore,
So near I could almost join in their play.
The rays from heaven,
The silver sea,
The dolphins at play.
Joy extraordinary filled my heart –
God blessed this moment and I could see.

Imagination Tale

Her nimble mind catches imagination by the tail.

She whirls it around until her story begins to flow.

Her words twinkle with delight in revealing the magic stories in her heart.

So dream like the vision she tells us:

Creatures that walk the earth, fairylike characters that do extraordinary deeds.

This wonderful child guides us into the world of innocence and delicious adventures.

I am enchanted and held captive as I follow her through a landscape of giggles, wonder and delight.

This is a grand blessing for this grandmother.

Leaving the Ball

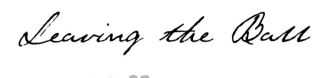

One of life's uneven edges is leaving the ball with the music still playing –
Blaring and unmelodic, it covers my emotions with confusion and bluster.
Into the quietness of the night, the full moon washes my thoughts with a
    calm and gentle glow;
I find an arbor of tranquility in the moonlit garden.
As I look up into the starry sky, my soul smiles easily.
I see the shadow of another enjoying the reverie of this moment.

Uneven Edges

Life seems to tumble us down a waterfall of uneven edges.
Our landscape has searing sun and lo, the balm of a soothing moon.
If we choose life, we walk through muddy loneliness,
Through tangled briars of sharp, unkind words
And greedy thieves stealing our innocence, our joy, our creative ideas.
The cold wind of rejection and love not returned –
Those uneven edges often bring fear and hopelessness.
Alas, our landscape also has gardens full of flowers and loving friends –
Streams of creativity and a twinkle that lights our way and entices us to
    march to our passion.
All ends well.

It's a Sweet Life if You're Drinking from the Loving Cup

Her Majesty Beauty floats atop a bubble drifting on a gasp of wonder.
Shower in the light of Beauty, and cover your eyes with her loveliness.
For in a heartbeat she darts into the past.
Oh, life, be gentle in the teaching of our daily lesson,
That the lilt of our laughter explodes as we discover the hidden flower of
   hope.
As the stones and brambles bruise and tear at our pride,
Let us shed this tattered worldly cloak.
Wearing only a simple covering that lets us dance freely to the music.
Seek a hand to hold and a shoulder to lean upon.
Fill your cup with only loving nectar – drink deep –
And share this cup of life with all who are sent your way.

Jubilation Juice

Squeally good – so happy that the jubilation juice just spews from my very
soul!

That goodness that I'm alive is so real that it tickles my fancy and makes me
laugh out loud.

I'm probably in the rocking chair and it's a summer day and I'm
remembering the hug, kiss and laughter of loved ones.

A day to live, a day to love, and a day to be thankful and have a cup of
jubilation juice and pass it all around.

Conclusion

In this time together, I have shared a few thoughts I have had these last few years. They have all come from my heart and my growing. In closing, I would like to share a quote that says how I feel: "When I stand before God at the end of my life, I would hope that I would not have a single bit of talent left, and I could say, 'I used everything you gave me.'" *(Erma Bombeck)*

Thank you for sharing in my cup of Jubilation Juice.

Acknowledgments

I wish to express my deep gratitude to Gardner Smith who gathered, organized, and typed these many pages correcting misspelled words and my generous lack of punctuation –

To my friends JoAnn, Phoebe and Grace who listened with love and encouragement –

To Ann Wells whose discerning eye proofread these pages with good humor –

To Florence who once again gave me a haven by the sea to spark my thoughts and quiet my heart –

To Kathy for typing these thoughts with caring and patience-Her loving heart is always by my side –

To Grace for her joyous and happy spirit and many hours of shared laughter –

To Alex, Kayce and Ginny who keep me young at heart and alert to life's wonders, the joy of innocent kindness and extraordinary hugs that keep my heart warm –

'The joy is Real'
Kay Lazenby